HAL LEONARD

EASY BANJO SOLOS

BERTSON

Welcome to *Easy Banjo Solos*, a collection of 16 timeless songs arranged for 5-string banjo. This beginner's songbook can be used on its own or as a supplement to the *Hal Leonard Banjo Method*, or any other beginning banjo method. The songs are arranged in order of difficulty and presented in an easy-to-follow format, with the melody line on the top staff and the banjo solo on the bottom staff.

The author gratefully acknowledges Jon Peik's assistance with arrangements.

ISBN 978-0-7935-2333-7

HAL•LEONARD®
CORPORATION

7777 W. BLUEMOUND RD. P.O. BOX 13819 MILWAUKEE, WI 53213

Visit Hal Leonard Online at
www.halleonard.com

TOM DOOLEY

Words and Music Collected, Adapted and Arranged by
Frank Warner, John A. Lomax and Alan Lomax
From the singing of Frank Proffitt

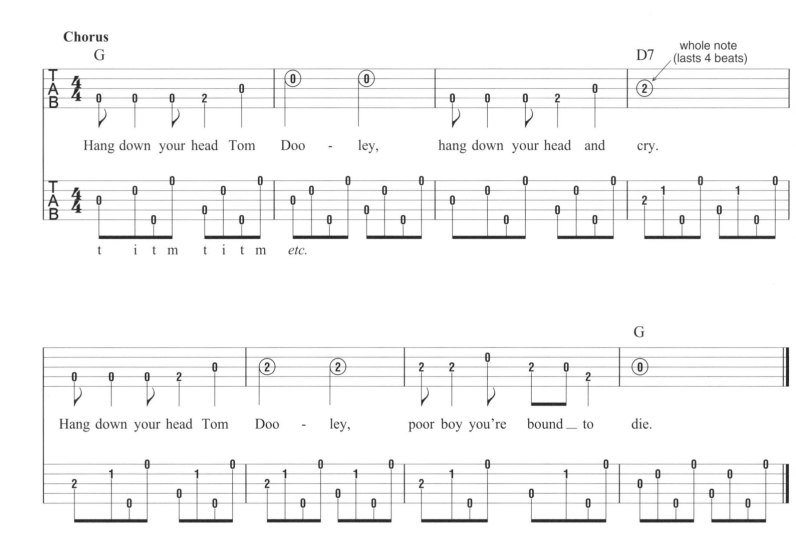

Additional Verses

1. Met her on the mountain,
   Said she'd be my wife,
   But the gal refused me,
   Stabbed her with my knife. *CHORUS*

2. 'Bout this time tomorrow
   Reckon where I'll be,
   Down in some lonesome valley
   Hanging from a big oak tree. *CHORUS*

ROCKY TOP

Words and Music by Boudleaux Bryant
and Felice Bryant

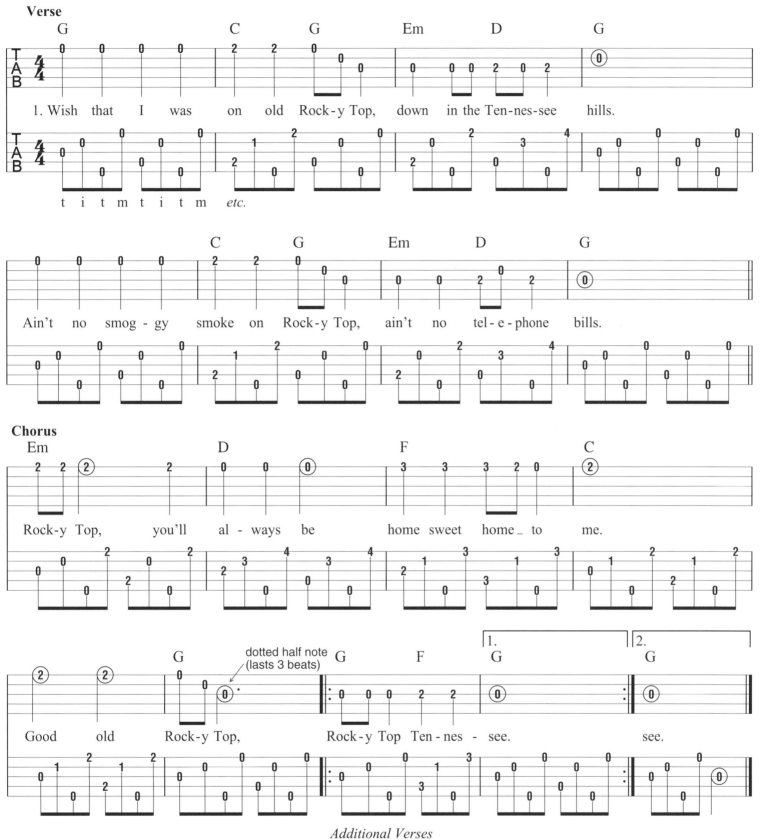

Additional Verses

2. Once two strangers climbed ol' Rocky Top lookin' for a moonshine still.
   Strangers ain't come down from Rocky Top; reckon they never will. *CHORUS*

3. Corn won't grow at all on Rocky Top; dirt's too rocky by far.
   That's why all the folks on Rocky Top get their corn from a jar. *CHORUS*

THIS LAND IS YOUR LAND

Words and Music by
Woody Guthrie

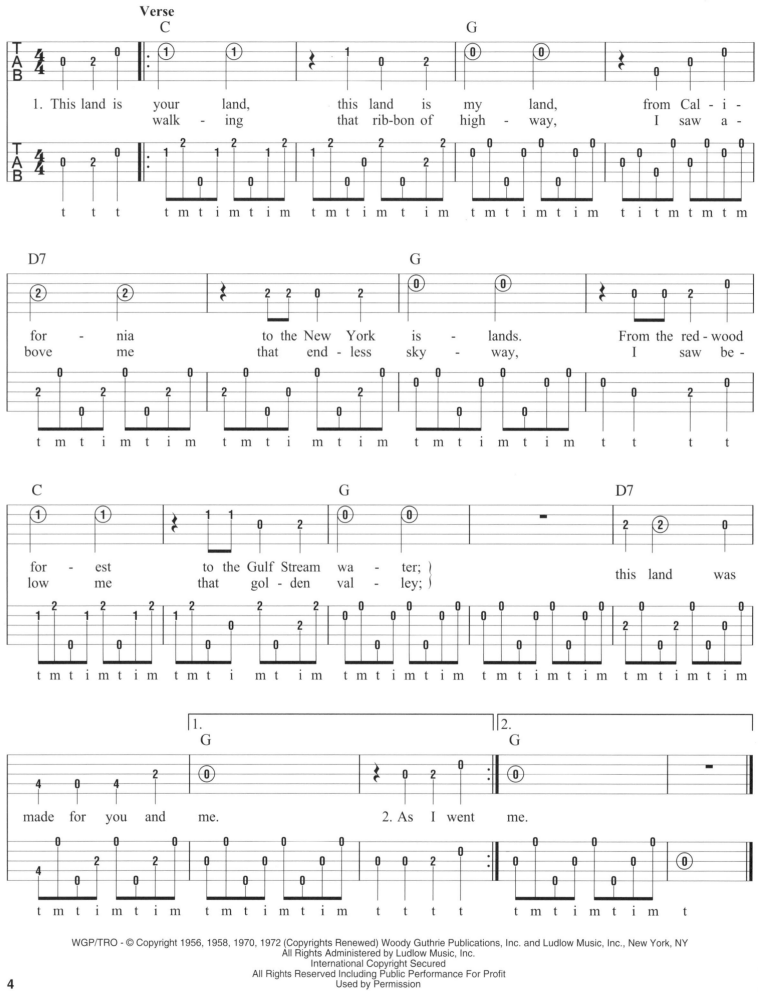

WABASH CANNONBALL

Words and Music by
A.P. Carter

Verse

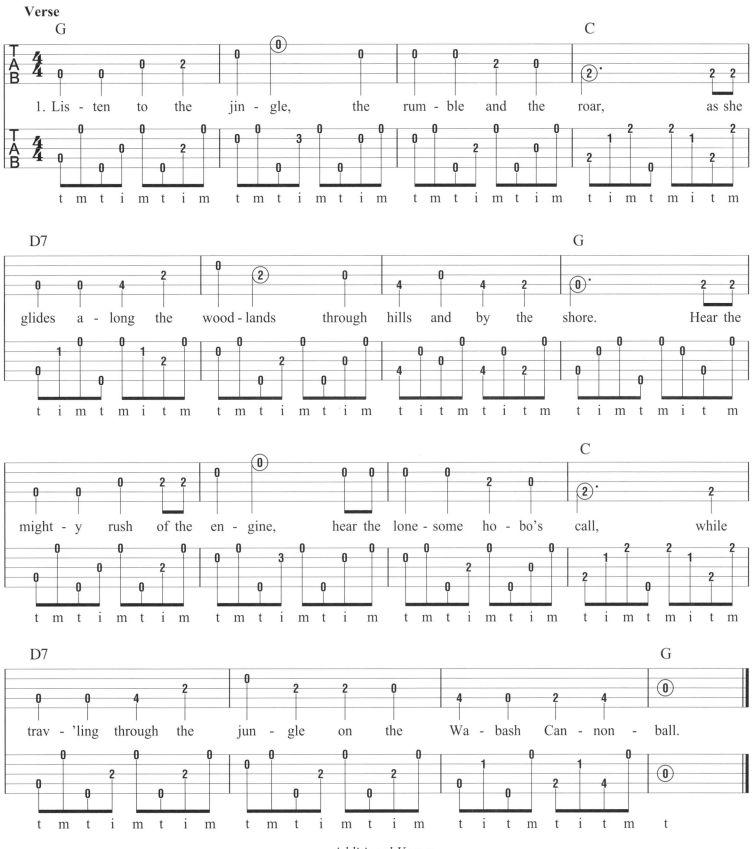

Additional Verses

2. Now the eastern states are dandy, so the western people say,
From New York to St. Louis and Chicago by the way.
From the hills of Minnesota where the rippling waters fall,
No changes can be taken on the Wabash Cannonball.

OH, LONESOME ME

Words and Music by
Don Gibson

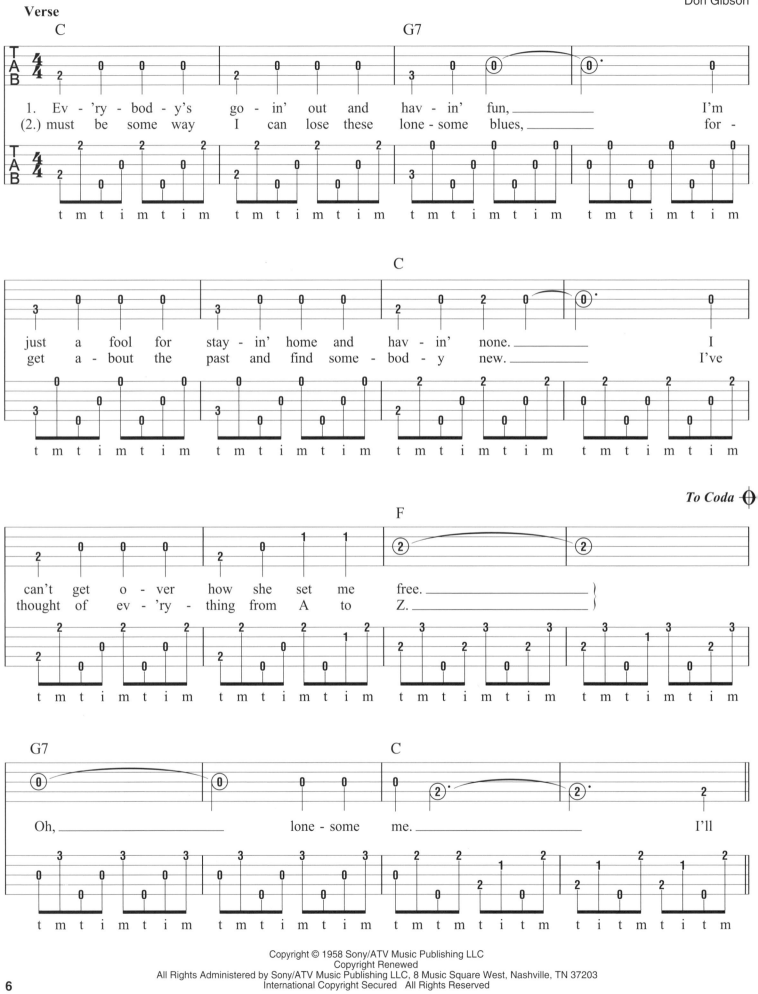

Bridge

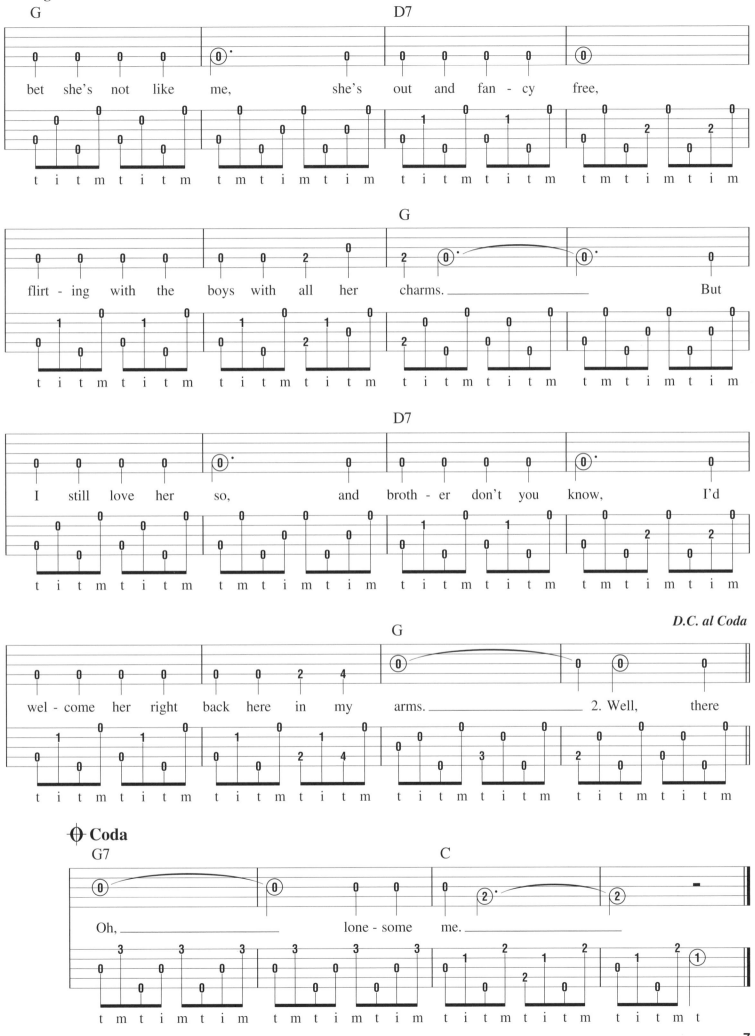

I'VE JUST SEEN A FACE

Words and Music by John Lennon
and Paul McCartney

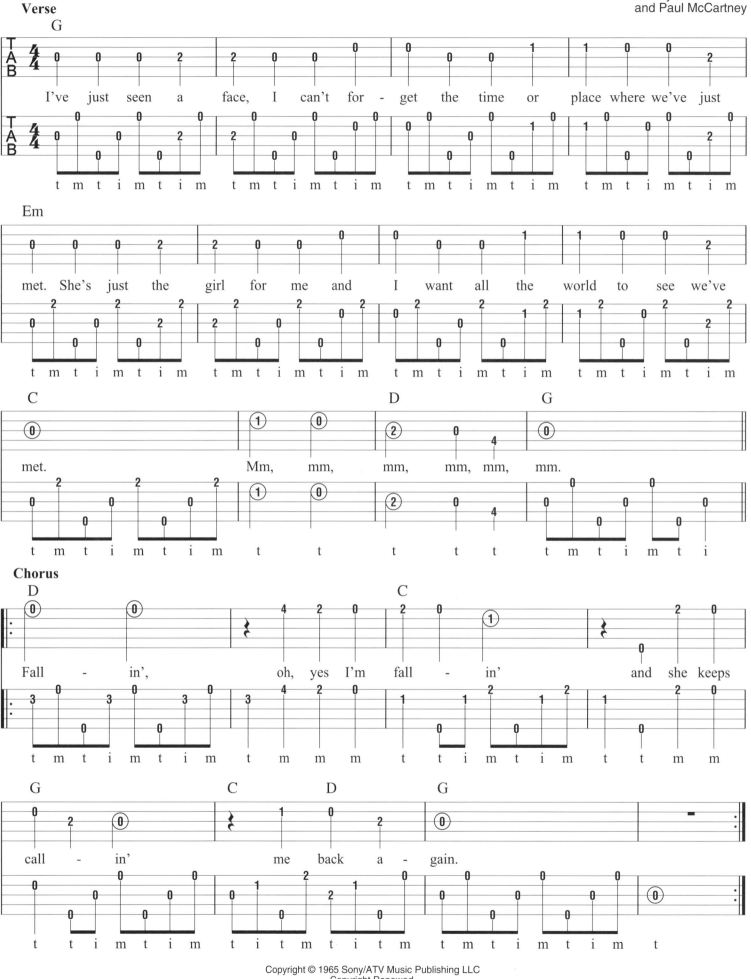

WILL THE CIRCLE BE UNBROKEN

Words by Ada R. Habershon
Music by Charles H. Gabriel

Chorus

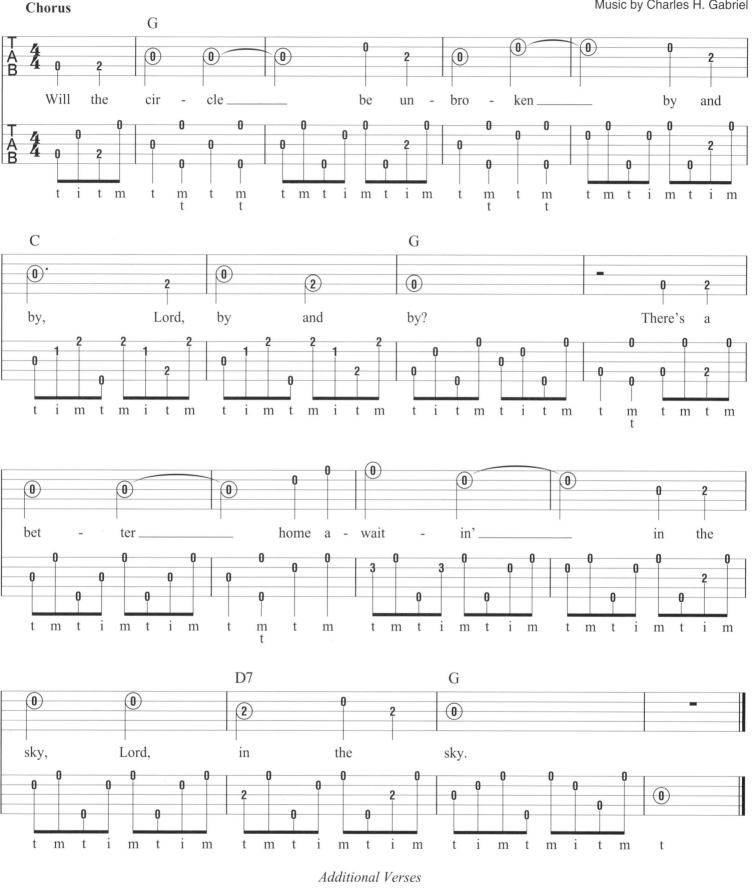

Additional Verses

1. I was standing by my window
   On a cold and cloudy day,
   When I saw that hearse come rolling
   For to carry my mother away. *CHORUS*

2. Lord, I told that undertaker
   Undertaker please drive slow,
   For this body that you're hauling
   Lord, I hate to see her go. *CHORUS*

3. I followed close behind her
   Tried to hold up and be brave,
   But I could not hide my sorrow
   When they laid her in the grave. *CHORUS*

BALLAD OF JED CLAMPETT

from the Television Series THE BEVERLY HILLBILLIES

Words and Music by Paul Henning

MOUNTAIN DEW

Words and Music by Scott Wiseman
and Bascomb Lunsford

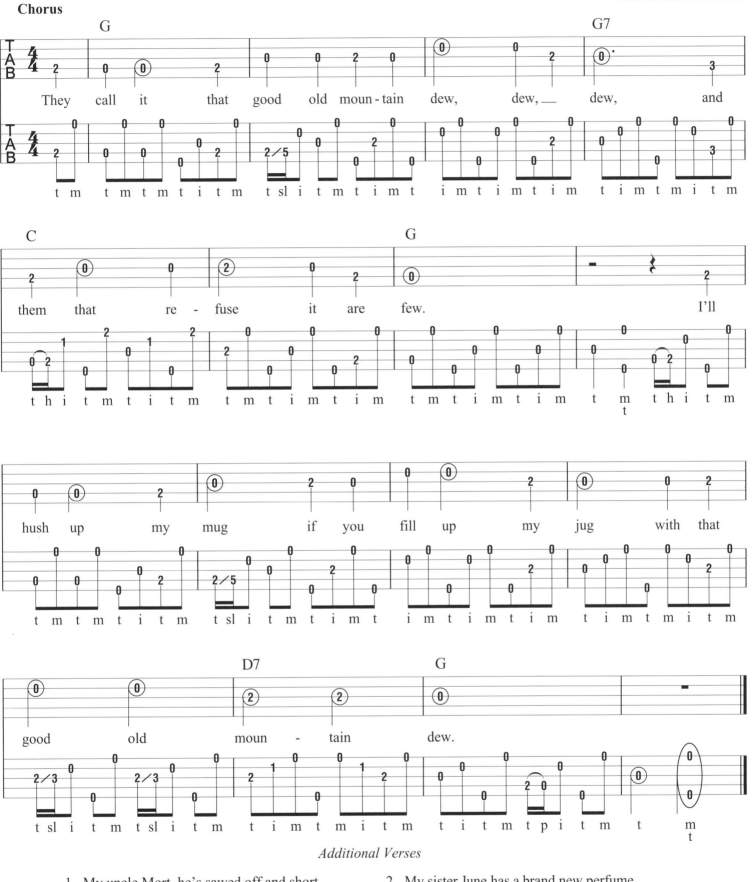

Additional Verses

1. My uncle Mort, he's sawed off and short,
   Measures about four foot two,
   But he thinks he's a giant if you give him a pint,
   Of that good old mountain dew.

2. My sister June has a brand new perfume
   It has a sweet-smelling p-u.
   Imagine her surprise when she had it analyzed,
   'Twas nothin' but good old mountain dew.

I'LL FLY AWAY

Words and Music by
Albert E. Brumley

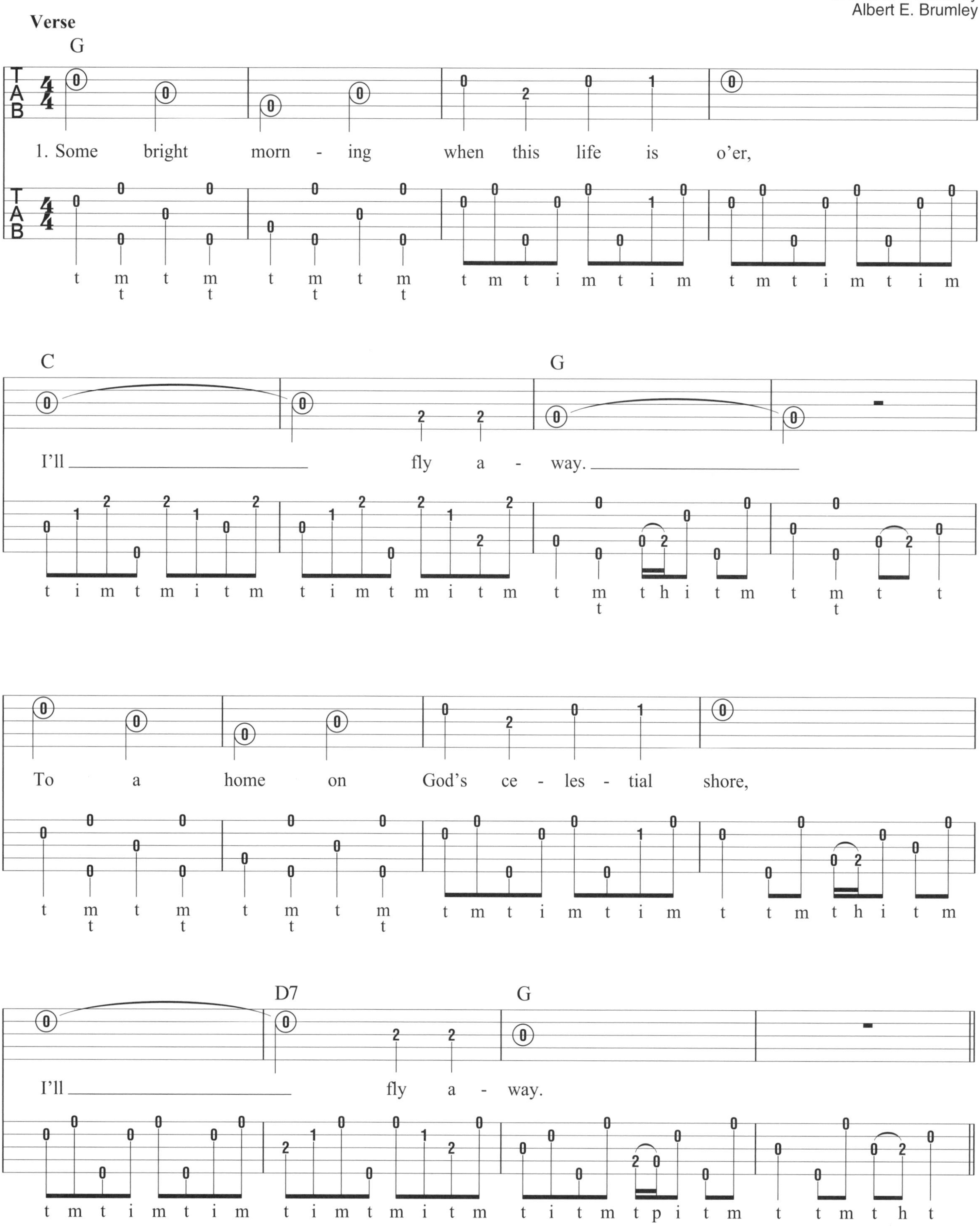

Verse

1. Some bright morn - ing when this life is o'er,

I'll _____ fly a - way. _____

To a home on God's ce - les - tial shore,

I'll _____ fly a - way.

Chorus

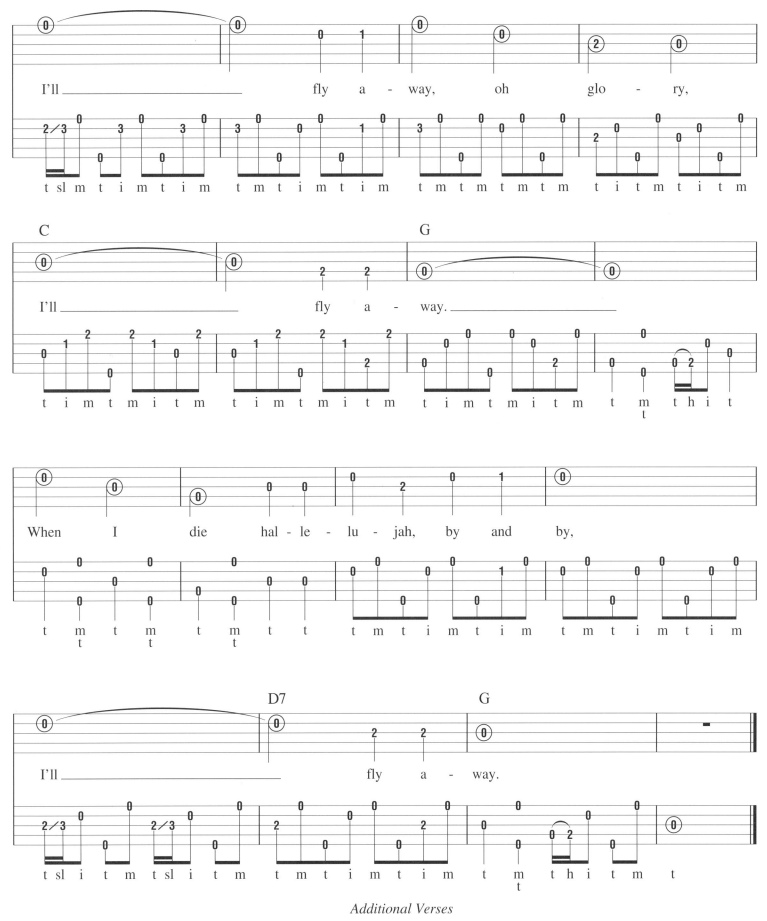

Additional Verses

1. When the shadows of this life have grown, I'll fly away.
   Like a bird that from prison bars has flown, I'll fly away. *CHORUS*

2. Just a few more weary days and then, I'll fly away.
   To a land where joy shall never end, I'll fly away. *CHORUS*

WAGON WHEEL

Words and Music by Ketch Secor
and Bob Dylan

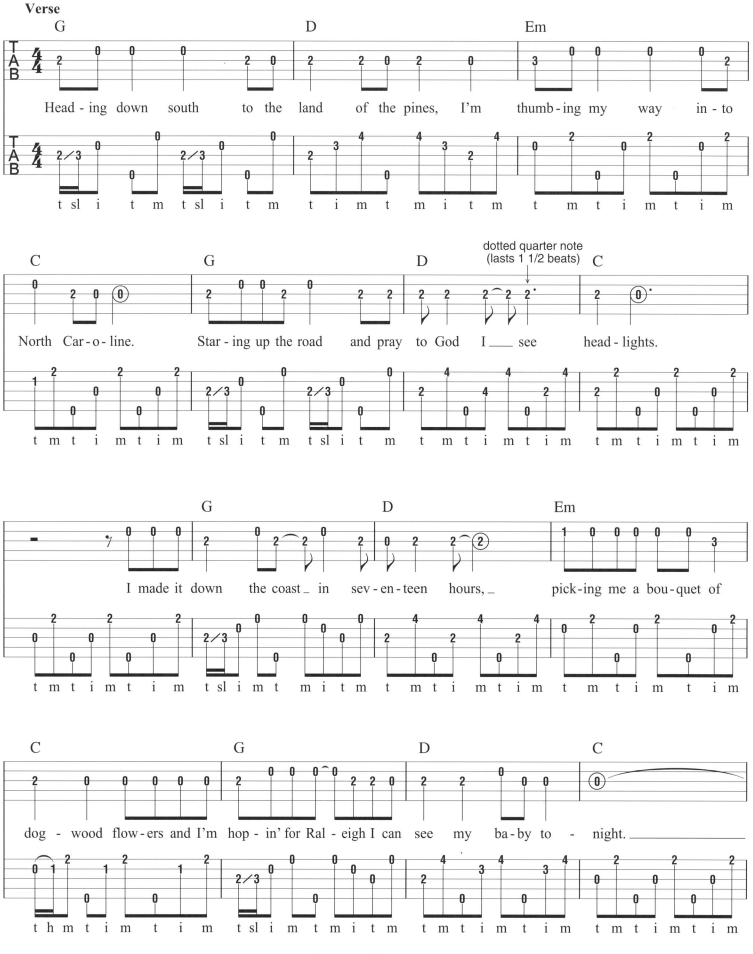

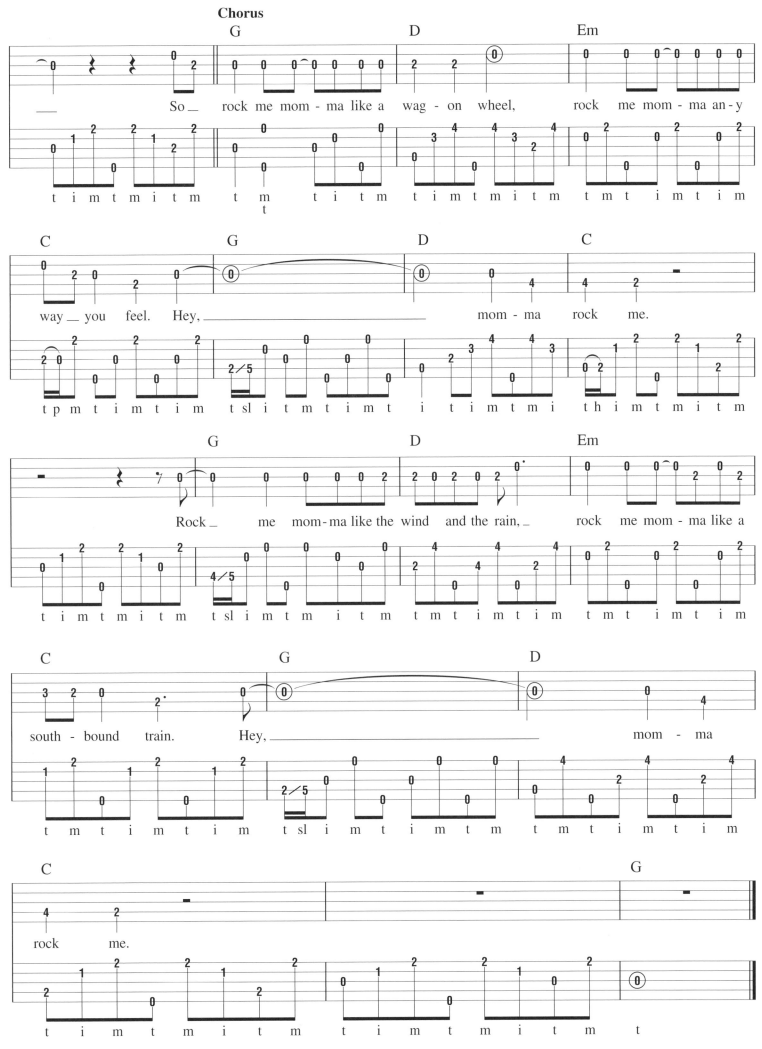

ASHOKAN FAREWELL

Theme from PBS Series THE CIVIL WAR

By Jay Ungar

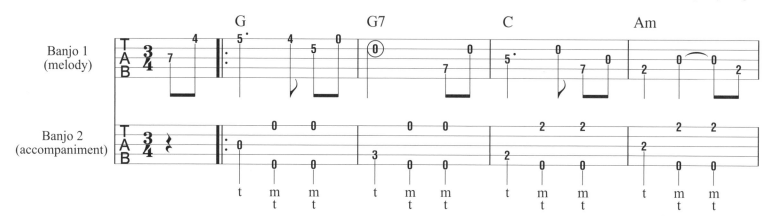

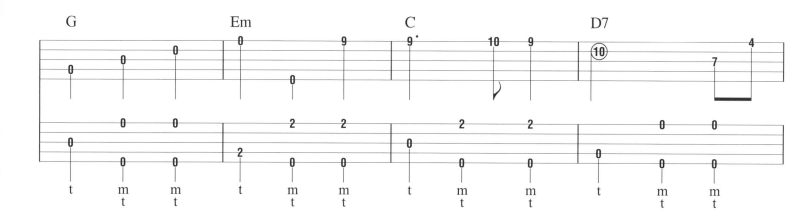

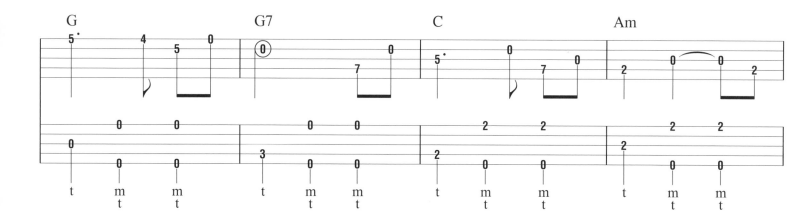

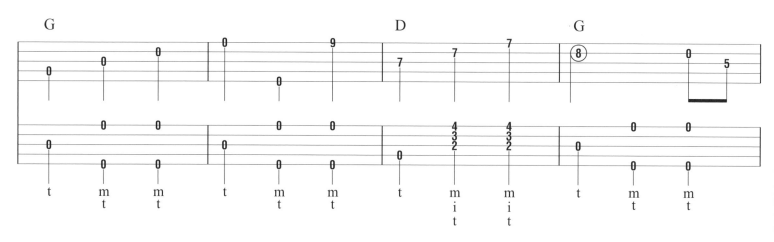

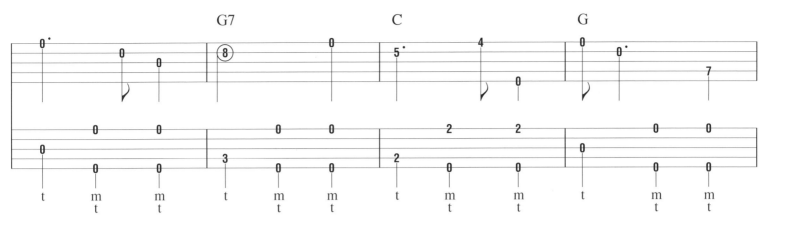

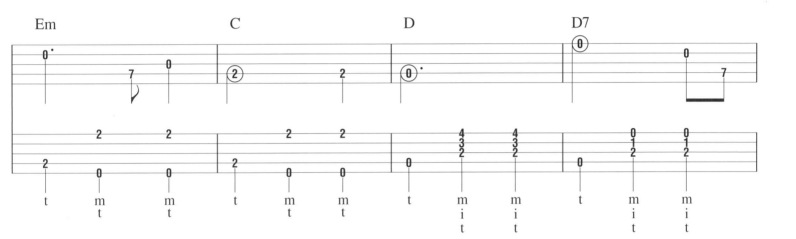

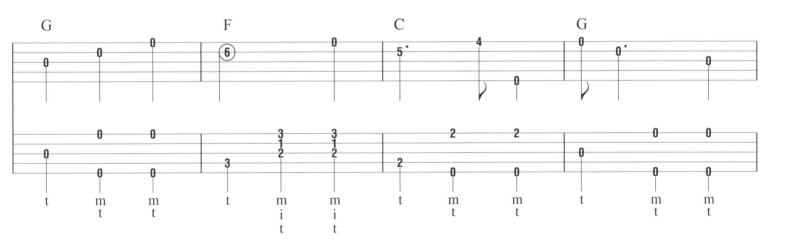

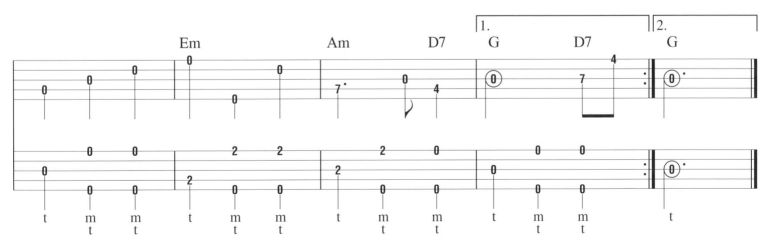

I SAW THE LIGHT

Words and Music by
Hank Williams

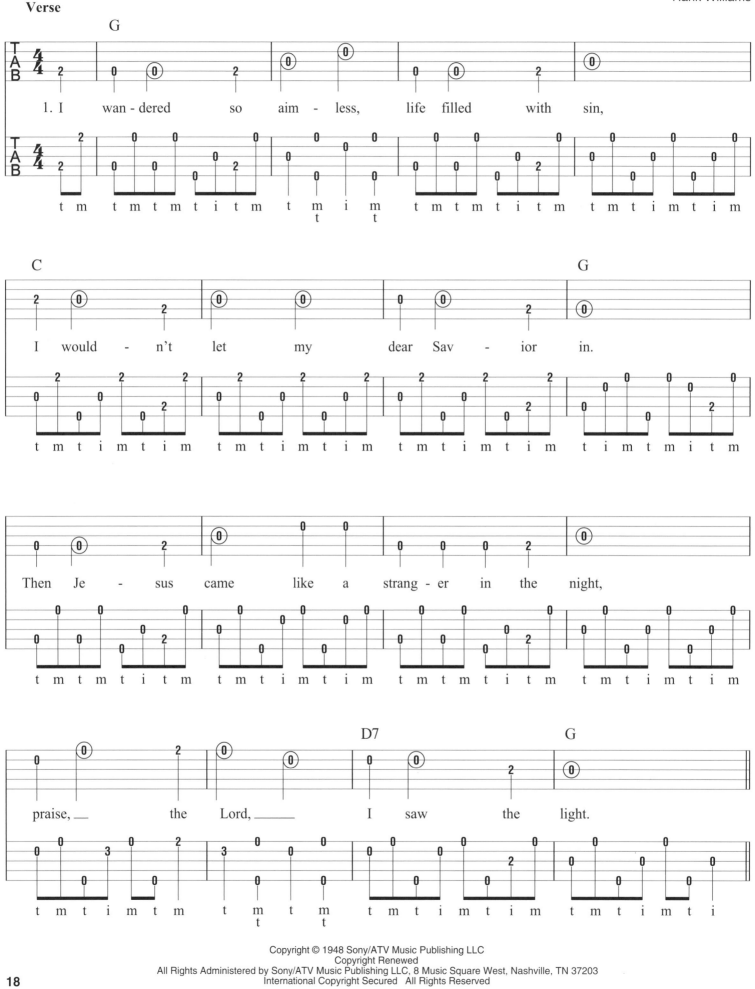

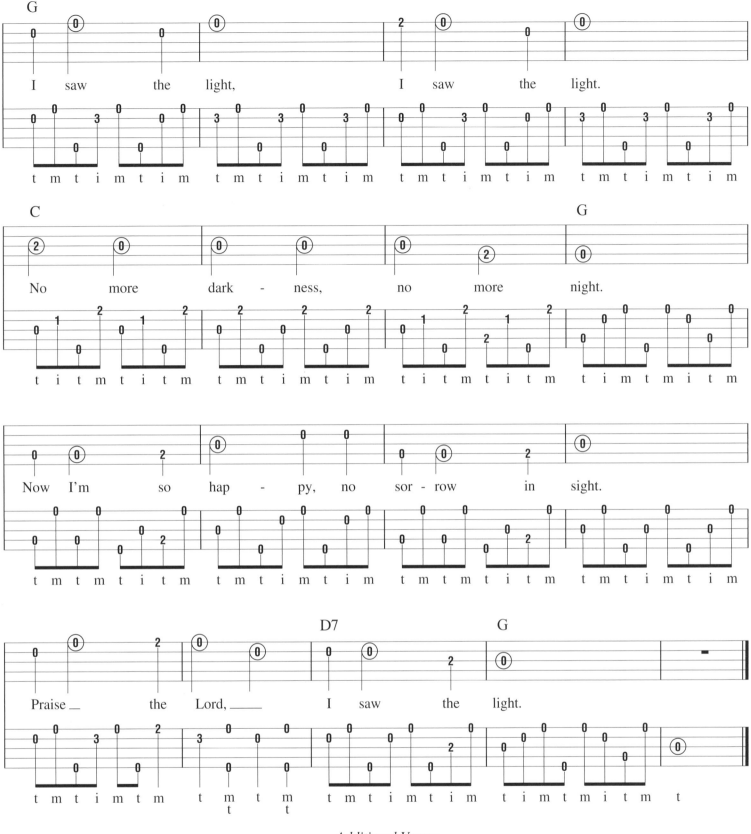

Additional Verses

2. Just like a blind man, I wandered alone.
   Worries and fears I claimed for my own.
   Then like the blind man that God gave back his sight,
   Praise the Lord, I saw the light. *CHORUS*

3. I was a fool to wander and stray.
   Straight is the gate and narrow the way.
   Now I have traded the wrong for the right,
   Praise the Lord, I saw the light. *CHORUS*

HEY, GOOD LOOKIN'

Words and Music by
Hank Williams

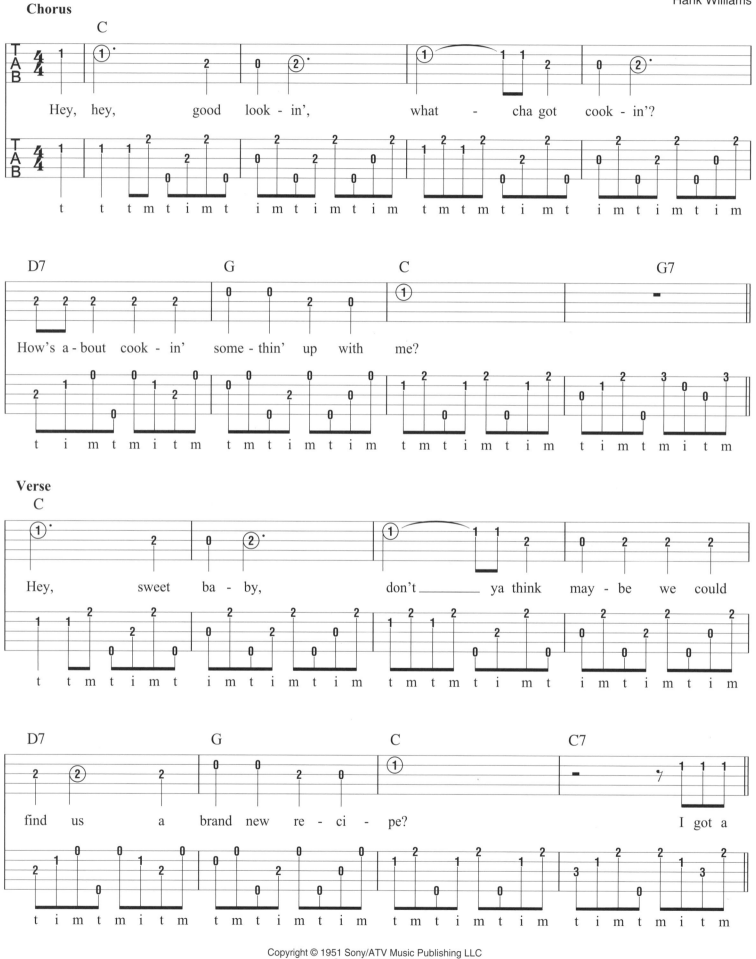

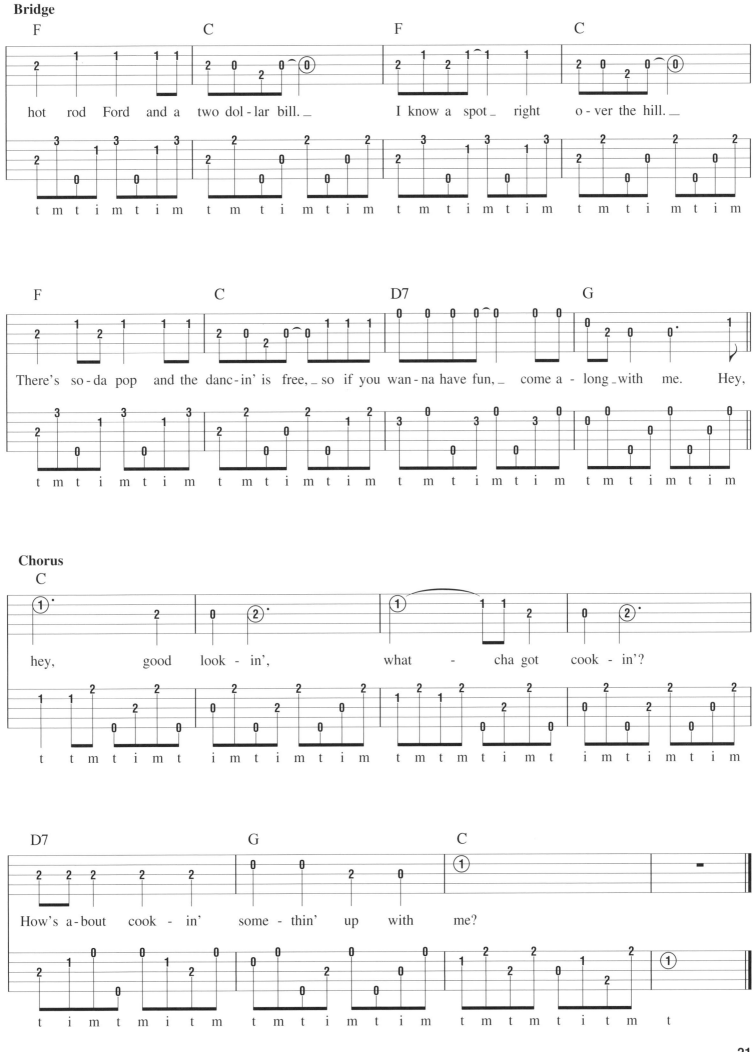

BLACK DIAMOND

Words and Music by
Don Stover

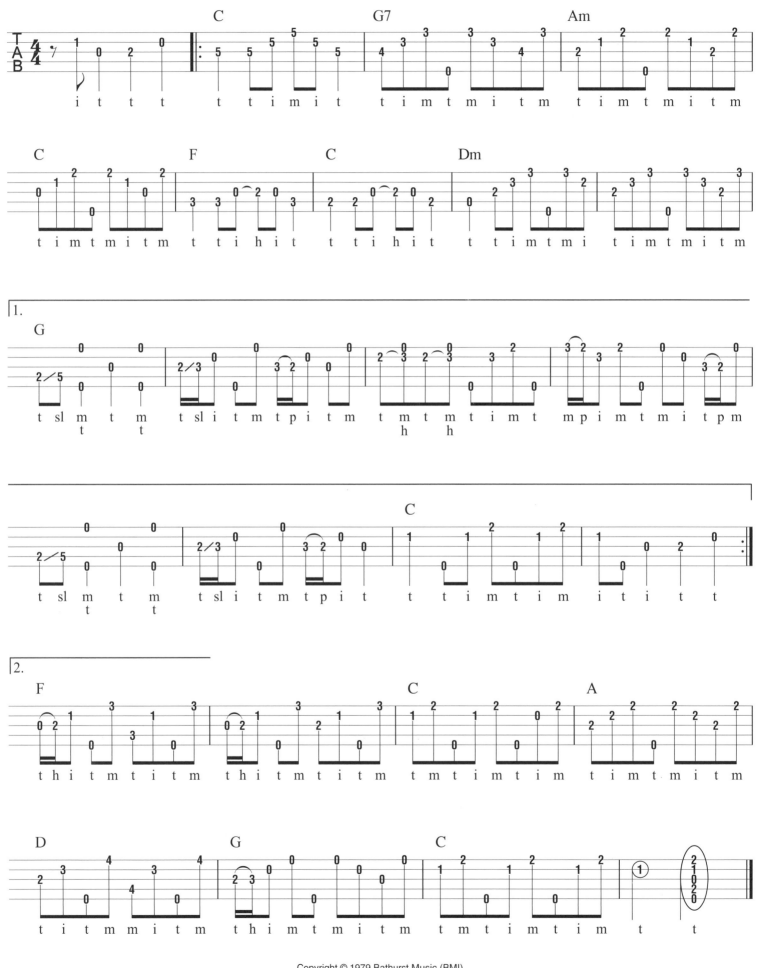

NINE POUND HAMMER

Words and Music by
Merle Travis

Verse

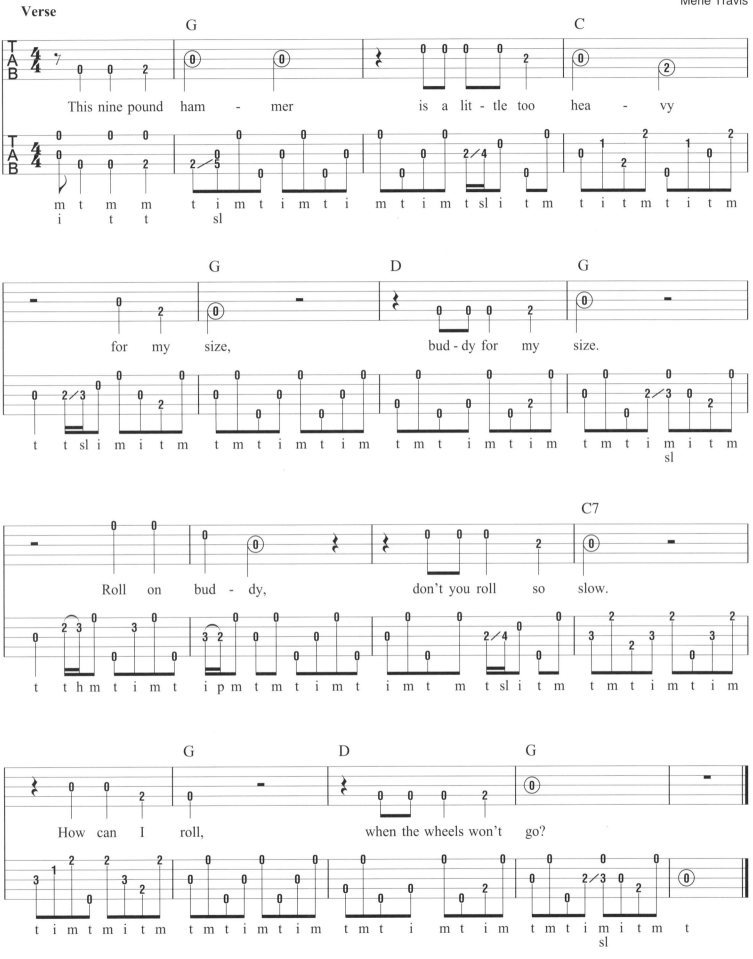

GREAT BANJO PUBLICATIONS

FROM HAL LEONARD

Hal Leonard Banjo Method

by Mac Robertson, Robbie Clement, Will Schmid

This innovative method teaches 5-string banjo bluegrass style using a carefully paced approach that keeps beginners playing great songs *while learning*. Book 1 covers easy chord strums, tablature, right-hand rolls, hammer-ons, slides and pull-offs, and more. Book 2 includes solos and licks, fiddle tunes, back-up, capo use, and more.

00699500 Book 1 Book Only $9.99
00695101 Book 1 Book/Online Audio $17.99
00699502 Book 2 Book Only $9.99

Banjo Chord Finder
00695741 9 x 12..$8.99
00695742 6 x 9..$7.99

Banjo Scale Finder
00695783 6 x 9..$6.99

Banjo Aerobics
A 50-Week Workout Program for Developing, Improving and Maintaining Banjo Technique
by Michael Bremer

Take your banjo playing to the next level with this fantastic daily resource, providing a year's worth of practice material with a two-week vacation. The accompanying audio includes demo tracks for all the examples in the book to reinforce how the banjo should sound.

00113734 Book/Online Audio $22.99

Earl Scruggs and the 5-String Banjo

Earl Scruggs' legendary method has helped thousands of banjo players get their start. It features everything you need to know to start playing, even how to build your own banjo! Topics covered include: Scruggs tuners • how to read music • chords • how to read tablature • anatomy of Scruggs-style picking • exercises in picking • 44 songs • biographical notes • and more! The online audio features Earl Scruggs playing and explaining over 60 examples!

00695764 Book Only $29.99
00695765 Book/Online Audio $39.99

First 50 Songs You Should Play on Banjo

arr. Michael J. Miles & Greg Cahill

Easy-to-read banjo tab, chord symbols and lyrics for the most popular songs banjo players like to play. Explore clawhammer and three-finger-style banjo in a variety of tunings and capoings with this one-of-a-kind collection. Songs include: Angel from Montgomery • Carolina in My Mind • Cripple Creek • Danny Boy • The House of the Rising Sun • Mr. Tambourine Man • Take Me Home, Country Roads • This Land Is Your Land • Wildwood Flower • and many more.
00153311 ....$15.99

Fretboard Roadmaps
by Fred Sokolow

This handy book/with online audio will get you playing all over the banjo fretboard in any key! You'll learn to: increase your chord, scale and lick vocabulary • play chord-based licks, moveable major and blues scales, melodic scales and first-position major scales • and much more! The audio includes 51 demonstrations of the exercises.

00695358 Book/Online Audio $17.99

The Great American Banjo Songbook
70 Songs
arr. Alan Munde & Beth Mead-Sullivan

Explore the repertoire of the "Great American Songbook" with this 70-song collection, masterfully arranged by Alan Munde and Beth Mead-Sullivan for 3-finger, Scruggs-style 5-string banjo. Rhythm tab, right hand fingerings and chord diagrams are included for each of these beloved melodies. Songs include: Ain't She Sweet • Blue Skies • Cheek to Cheek • Home on the Range • Honeysuckle Rose • It Had to Be You • Little Rock Getaway • Over the Rainbow • Sweet Georgia Brown • and more.
00156862 ....$19.99

How to Play the 5-String Banjo
Third Edition
by Pete Seeger

This basic manual for banjo players includes melody line, lyrics and banjo accompaniment and solos notated in standard form and tablature. Chapters cover material such as: a basic strum, the fifth string, hammering on, pulling off, double thumbing, and much more.

14015486 ....$19.99

O Brother, Where Art Thou?

Banjo tab arrangements of 12 bluegrass/folk songs from this Grammy-winning album. Includes: The Big Rock Candy Mountain • Down to the River to Pray • I Am a Man of Constant Sorrow • I Am Weary (Let Me Rest) • I'll Fly Away • In the Jailhouse Now • Keep on the Sunny Side • You Are My Sunshine • and more, plus lyrics and a banjo notation legend.

00699528 Banjo Tablature $17.99

Clawhammer Cookbook
Tools, Techniques & Recipes for Playing Clawhammer Banjo
by Michael Bremer

The goal of this book isn't to tell you how to play tunes or how to play like anyone else. It's to teach you ways to approach, arrange, and personalize any tune – to develop your own unique style. To that end, we'll take in a healthy serving of old-time music and also expand the clawhammer palate to taste a few other musical styles. Includes audio track demos of all the songs and examples to aid in the learning process.
00118354 Book/Online Audio $22.99

The Ultimate Banjo Songbook

A great collection of banjo classics: Alabama Jubilee • Bye Bye Love • Duelin' Banjos • The Entertainer • Foggy Mountain Breakdown • Great Balls of Fire • Lady of Spain • Orange Blossom Special • (Ghost) Riders in the Sky • Rocky Top • San Antonio Rose • Tennessee Waltz • UFO-TOFU • You Are My Sunshine • and more.

00699565 Book/Online Audio $29.99

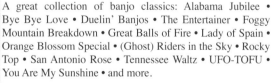

Prices, contents, and availability subject to change without notice.